PIRENE'S
FOUNTAIN

PIRENE'S FOUNTAIN

VOLUME 15, ISSUE 23

Pirene's Fountain: A Journal of Poetry
Volume 15, Issue 23
Copyright © 2022 Pirene's Fountain
Paperback ISSN 2331-1096

Editor: Megan Merchant
Layout, Book & Cover Design: Steven Asmussen
Cover Artist: © Juliscalzi | Dreamstime.com

All rights reserved: except for the purpose of quoting brief passages for review, no part of this book may be reproduced or transmitted in any form or by any means, electronic or mechanical, including photocopying, recording, or by any information storage and retrieval system, without permission in writing from the publisher.

Glass Lyre Press, LLC
P.O. Box 2693
Glenview, IL 60025

www.GlassLyrePress.com

Contents

Poetry

Francesca Bell
Rhubarb — 9
Two Stories — 10

Ace Boggess
A Fuse Pops — 11
Prison Years — 12

Rebecca Brock
Late Winter Glaze — 13
The Mother Considers Solastalgia — 14
Tiger — 16

Lauren K. Carlson
Impatiens — 17
Providence Township, Lac Qui Parle, Minnesota — 18

Julia Chiapella
Delirium — 19
Four Days In Portland, Late July — 20

H. Lee Coakley
Requiem for a Burning Planet — 22
Kaddish — 24

Steven Deutsch
Coffee Shop — 27

Sherine Gilmour
Ferocious Machine — 29

Joan Kwon Glass
Even the Moon — 31
Middle School Pastoral — 32

Max Heinegg
Afterlife — 33

Tim Kahl
The Principles of Traffic — 34

Jen Karetnick
Mo(u)rning Crow — 36

Jane Rosenberg LaForge
The After Plants — 37
Reception — 38

Katie Manning
    Choosing a Moon   39
    This Poem is About Dinosaurs   41

Norman Minnick
    Steger & Sons   42
    The Show Must   43

Richard Oyama
    The House at the End of a Road   44
    Calligraphy   45

Dave Shumate
    In the Age of Losses   46
    In the Presence of Children   47

Neil Silberblatt
    Right of Return   48
    Modern Times   49

Meghan Sterling
    Animal Dreams   51
    Rear-View   52

Susan Terris
    Buffalo Jump   54
    The Purkapile Test   55

Cindy Veach
    Artifact   56
    How to Mourn a Dead Icelandic Glacier from Massachusetts   57
    I Dressed My Salad with Sadness   58

Allison Wilkins
    Nausicaa, Agora   59

Reviews

I Was a Bell by M. Soledad Caballero (Red Hen Press, 2021)   63
    Reviewed by Elizabeth Nichols

Prompts
Contributor Notes

POETRY

Rhubarb

Francesca Bell

I.

Sometimes cooking is like being
with you. Uncovering each layer,
onions knife my eyes. I was a girl
watching you in the kitchen.
You taught me to peel back the delicate
skin, to make the pieces small.
Cooking, it's okay to cry
when life bubbles beneath your masked face,
bitter as rhubarb stewing on the stove.
Even sugar doesn't erase the taste
passed from your mouth to mine.

II.

Peeling peaches, I remember
your slight weight against the edge
of sink and think, if you had moved,
the house would have fallen
around us. My own sink
is cool now, hard against the hollow
my hips make. Peach skins gash
its white surface. Divided, bare,
the fruit smells like you.
I see the darkness of each half
bleeding out from the center.

Two Stories

Francesca Bell

In the dream, Mother, we live in two stories
near a field parched white, and you know
the field will come alive with fire,
and fire will flicker to our house
and consume it completely. Yet you say
I may not go up the stairs and bring out
my boxes of poems or carry my cat
with gold eyes from the treacherous
rooms. You refuse to help me carry
my books or pictures of me at every age
or the painting of the red-haired girl praying.
I run fast as I can to each house, begging
for someone to help me save what I have saved
of the years of my life. But no one moves
fast enough. So I come to stand with you,
Mother, and watch as our house lights up,
a blaze dancing through every room.
I must stand there knowing
each green plant I have watered folds
in on itself, and my face in the photograph
of my fourth birthday blisters and weeps
down the page. I must listen and clearly hear
my own voice, my poems hissing in the flames.

A Fuse Pops

Ace Boggess

Light greens brightly into vanishing.
Now the house is dark, street dark, dark
the stairs, mailbox, & vehicles.

One feels loneliest in dead moments
as if choosing between companionship &
mausoleum, a raucous party &

the crypt, hands of a lover brushing cheeks &
the lid of a coffin through which
he or she can't see.

Flipping switches in a void, one seeks
the fault, hoping isolation will be brief;
this loss, for the loser, less than grief.

Prison Years

Ace Boggess

Rewind my head searching for one line
I haven't written about time
reduced to a five-digit number hand-
sewn on khaki shirts. It's all there.
Why do I go back? Why seek out
ugly nights for a memory I missed?
Wasn't it enough to live each moment
twice? *More, more,* the old me pleads,
squeezing a rock for juice. Some days
a drop lands on my cheek.

Late Winter Glaze

Rebecca Brock

It stays to trace each thing—the maple,
winter bare against sky,
the clustered shoots of jonquil,
the tulips just beginning, the
barren crape myrtle, the spruce
thick with evergreen.

It is easy to see emptiness,
to pass a thing and not see
how beauty might hold.

But think—
to give yourself, like that,
to something—
to trace invisible,
to exist transparent
but able, still
to light through, to make
some temporary thing seen,
beautiful
as any bright spring.

The Mother Considers Solastalgia

Rebecca Brock
Cape Hatteras, North Carolina

She squints to watch the seagulls
form scattered clouds around a trawler
just past the waves: two pelicans fly in tandem—
closer still, a rookery of cormorants:
swift dark bodies, bold suited for their world of wet.
Yesterday, she told her sons to look away
from the injured one,
flailing in the sand,
that awful terror and try of wings.
Behind her, seaside houses rise up
on delicate stilts. Over the ocean she hears
the noise of men rebuilding roads,
bridges that arch higher, reaching
to connect land to land that will not last—
even the cormorant was dying,
or trying not to,
on a stretch of disappearing sand
between Sound and Sea.
Today, she watches her children
build an ornate, crooked sandcastle,
their father adds flourishes
of engineering, details of seashell.
She knows they drove too far,
for too short a time—
tells herself an old, parental tale:
This, this is what they will remember.
She knows it isn't only pain and fear
that made that dying bird pulse and struggle—
also instinct, also memory: maybe
the feathered body's low swoop
through waves crashing, maybe beating wings

of brethren on the seascape, maybe
all those sleek iridescent lives,
each bearing out.

Tiger

Rebecca Brock

When I found myself mother
to a boy who would be
interested in tigers,
if there were any
nearby enough to catch,
I began to look for crevices and cracks,
the deep falls, sudden
implausibility, like a boy's tiger trap:
meat just out of reach,
the whisper sound
of padded paws on leaves
without ground beneath them—
that *whoosh*
of disappearance
that fearful maw
that shaky disbelief
not unlike when there is a baby new,
born, he and I still trembling, still wet,
the orientation—
happens in a moment—
for a tiger, maybe,
but I floundered, there,
at the changes
at the loss—caught
by how little I knew
of tigers, or falls, or
the possibilities
of little boys.

IMPATIENS

Lauren K. Carlson

In October the south wind came, force
out of season, and disruptive. The intrusion

kept alive what should not have been kept. Impatiens.
Should have been season of cold. Instead

south wind's gales against everything. Against
branches, gates, sails. In the freshwater

sea there were waves, now breaking against opposing waves.
The surf the south brings. Humidity delights

what will ultimately suffer the hard freeze. Impatiens.
The riptide will pull you away from shore,

and no one is strong enough to overcome its current.
Swim out and not against. Swim out then back toward shore.

In other words, once you've relented, you've got strength
to return. The seed pouch bursts when touched—the slightest touch.

Providence Township, Lac Qui Parle, Minnesota

Lauren K. Carlson

Imagine a night that's pure dark, where there are stars
only sometimes and no illuminated roads home.

Picture the remarkable absence of artificial light.
Half asleep you think you'd left a lamp on or worse,

didn't blow out the wilting candle in the dining room
before you headed to bed, only to finally figure

out the flickering is the curtain casting shadows, furnace air
hushing up from the heat register below, and the lace

interrupts the moonlight coming through the window.
Outside November leaves circle December's surface, snow

and, like a gray steeple against a grayer night, still,
still the way a magnifying glass in its stillness condenses

heat, a snowy owl. For the white winter hare, for you
this scene invites:

disease.

DELIRIUM

JULIA CHIAPELLA

The way   the hand brushes, zipper against
skin, gasping the breath.

The way   the dog writhes on her back, head tilted
to opening sky.

The way   Albinoni's "Adagio in G minor" suspends
sorrow, suspends everything.

The way   my father's body lay, jaw slack, footnote
to the story I continue.

The way   osprey glides over water, mirror
to its hunger.

The way   dirt trail winds through manzanita, bay,
eviscerating time.

The way   your body left mine—one whole, one
ripped, the cleaving of it.

Four Days In Portland, Late July

Julia Chiapella

There are just three beds in your front yard,
but I'm jealous of every one. Here we are—

friends for 44 years, and all that time you've
enchanted me. Returning home, two states

away, I am bewitched—my garden paltry
and spare, bereft of the bees in your flower

beds: mason, leafcutter, sweat, wool
carder, bumble—black-tailed, fuzzy-horned,

californicus—you identify every one, show
me how the wool carder strips the fuzz

off dusty lambs' ears, gathers it to its
belly: nesting material for the young; share

the new book on pollinators you found
at the workshop (the one you left early,

just as the group activity was set
to start). In the space of six years, you

lost a father and two sisters, yet this
joy in your garden, this Eden, this slice

of tenacious life you've carved, pierces:
a blunt-earned tenderness on a half

acre in the middle of a city crowing
with condos and cars. I am buzzing with

the bright brunt of it, shifting in my seat,
drifting with summer's slant in my eyes—

I wanted to stay. I wanted to drop
everything, turn acolyte, mendicant,

fetch water, let the hum of invertebrates
dazzle, scrape soft filaments from my breast.

As I drove away, you threw rose petals
at the windshield. They clung there for miles.

Requiem for a Burning Planet

H. Lee Coakley

*

every act is an atom.
birthed in the black hole of
chance & sent spinning,
wildly, out

past the troposphere,
out where our weather prolapses the polar vortex
& farther

*

A rising tympany of desperate language
& still,
what we crave stays
unnamable -

combusting in the electric night,
      splintering for want of touch,

praying like the ancients
for just a little more time.

& with luck,
one day,
      our fillings will line a satellite

*

does heartbreak imprint language? or the other way?
I want, I say & I am no closer to the meaning.

meaning is the fever we cannot break.

KADDISH

H. Lee Coakley

here,

        put out your hands.
        you want to get

clean.

every room in the hospital -
every doorway - leaves itself

*

open here,

there is still skin and blood
and sinew underneath.

the heart monitor still beeps
its dirty promise.

*

we are surfing the blood, now
      don't get lost.

it's a
tremendous amphitheater,
    but

        Oh,

what a rush.

*

there is a limit to what the human mind can
wipe away, there is a

terminal velocity to the heart that's crashing
through these sheets,

its sound coursing all the way down -
beyond you.

*

we stay alive from the toes up, it seems. blue

toes are a bad sign,
you've never checked,
        only felt the blank in the air as it stilled.

that was that and it didn't even disturb the sheets.

*

earlier today, the sky wrung itself out.

from the window, the branch and its finches are precise.

*

we are surfing the hall now,
stay steady.

the thin breeze hits like a door to its own escape and
you

        are still here.

the sky is blameless, its palms are empty

*

        your body
        without margin
        washed through
        by the white of the air

Coffee Shop

Steven Deutsch

It was not a hang-out
for either of us.
Just a coffee shop
half a block from First National.
A place to get out of the weather.

When the heatwave broke
the storm came in like Man o' War.
I remember my first thought
on seeing her—"Am I that wet?"
But she recognized me right off,
as if age and gravity

had not had their way.
Everyone thought we would marry—
but we had blown apart
the summer the cities burned—
the year Vietnam
was a nightmare for the wide awake.

Conversation stalled—
after all,
what was I to make
of her—
a woman now
whom I would never know?

We accept the ravages of time
a mirror presents,
but what of the gulfs
engendered?

The rain stopped.
We went our separate ways—
tonight, I would scan the old memories
like watching reruns of a favorite show
canceled for reasons lost long ago.

Ferocious Machine

Sherine Gilmour

When I envisioned parenting, I did not know
anything about this: waiting on the street

to strap my child into a government seat,
straps laden with strangers' saliva,

crumbs from other children's broken-down snacks,
to be ferried where specialists assess and analyze.

Each morning awakes like an unanswered question:
Will you speak? Will you keep

speaking? Will you lose your voice?
Each morning awakes like a cryptic message:

How are you? I do not know.
I constantly check your forehead while we wait.

What if you have a fever? What if
you are dehydrated? It's happened before.

Will these teachers—who say they are specialists
but have turned out more like babysitters,

some merely there for weeks willing to change
diapers of special-needs kids for $8 an hour—

will they know
how to take care of my child? He holds

my finger in his grasp.
How I hate the face of that bus.

At any moment, it will turn the corner,
lurch toward us.

Even the Moon

Joan Kwon Glass

My mother has never had alcohol
and never finishes her dessert.
Sometimes I wonder if this is why we
can't understand each other.
She wants a daughter so small,
the night won't claim her.
I want to know a version of her
that consumes more than her body wants,
insists on being uncomfortably full.
I devour the sweets she rejects
with a wave of the hand
and an *oh, I couldn't possibly!*
Have you ever seen a bird pick through
a bowl of seeds, pecking and scattering them
with such fury
that there are more on the cage floor
than in her own belly?
Have you ever met a mother
who was not a cage?
In her womb, I swelled as close to the surface
of her as I could without breaking through.
Maybe I'm the way I am because I need to know
how much my seams can hold.
Even the moon slivers herself.

Middle School Pastoral

Joan Kwon Glass

Every day whiteboards are filled with problems.
We do our best to solve them. We wipe them clean.
Rows of beakers glisten on science lab window sills,
clarinets and violins thump gently in their cases
as students carry them up and down stairs.
This month art classes have pinned portraits
of teachers to bulletin boards. Crafted in pixels,
their familiar faces somehow more themselves
when taken apart and pieced back together.
In May, a bumblebee wanders in through an open
window and the quietest girl in class scoops it
into her cupped palms, releases it without saying a word.
One day after recess my student brings me a leaf,
lays it in my hand as if he's found a robin's egg.
He says he's named it "Larry" and we fasten it
to the bulletin board next to photos of my children.
When it finally crumbles weeks later, we hold
a leaf funeral on a too-bright morning,
the kind of morning when a classroom transforms
into a palace of light and the school's unremarkable
linoleum maze seems to hold secret passageways.
Our elegy and laughter echoed by distant birdsong,
we sprinkle Larry into a white envelope,
promise to remember him forever.

AFTERLIFE

MAX HEINEGG

At the border, our presence was questioned
& deigned justified. We drove on
to find the City of Saints
through a barren hour of fields, then odd
rows of tiny Christmas trees
beside family farms closely joined
silos in winter sun & the tragicomic
temperature. Despite, birds gathered
to share the cold or taunt the hardy
conception of ourselves, the American myth
workers endure for Heaven's reward—
the Greeks told normal souls they were
destined to become leaves, flitting
in the grey meadows of Asphodel,
unsettled by wind. Weakling shades
not dark enough to warrant Furies'
whips or any depth of Tartarus,
& not the warlike bright who died
without dying to sleep in the Elysian
Fields beneath their own constellations.
Just leaves who take the name of shades,
& worst, no memory—the streams of Lethe
steal everything. There's no keeping
the look you're giving, the one
that took my life to see.

The Principles of Traffic

Tim Kahl

Who will take down the campaign signs
now that the election is over?
They stand off to the side of the lanes that merge
onto the highway, good for one last eyeball salute.
We drive by and sneer in side glance,
marveling at all that useless provocation.
They're like a piano that's grown too big
for its room. Once the music used to agitate
the soul. Now a team of men must be
summoned for its removal. All that money
spent to bring it there and on lessons for
the kids. It seems a goddamned shame,
especially when not even a hint of Chopin
ever dared to enter there. I see another
prominent grove of them as I take my exit
to stand in front of a classroom of students.
I lecture about a country where there
is public financing, real spending limits,
transparency of donors, just a month-long
struggle and then it's all over. But no one
is paying attention. They're all on their phones
wooed by videos or professionally designed
displays, and I am armed with pitiful word.
It's sad to think I was raised on TV and
they were raised on YouTube. Both of us
ruined, our reasoning rendered helpless
in front of the moving image. Today
my thinking is so broken I make myself
believe that if I wheel a grand piano
into class, someone in there will be
the next Keith Jarrett, enthrall us with
his world of talent, his promise and wisdom,

play the whole Köln Concert note for note.
The music again will fill up the room,
maybe leak out onto the highways
where the radios still play and drivers
can exercise their will according to
the principles of traffic.

Mo(u)rning Crow

Jen Karetnick

After Morning Crow *by Martha Worthy*

Note the developing, telescoping scowl that says
how nobody likes being up quite this early, so cast a tired
stone at that myth about birds and joy-song. A crow is just a
crab dressed in completely different armor, but still

claws are always in motion in search of toes that
are for taking or troubling news that can be snatched and
delivered like pieces of silver. True, we see omens everywhere
now but who can blame us? We don't need Poe's raven

to give a name to that earthworm feeling squirming in
our benthic guts, to remind us that we can't sleep in our
own beds without worrying that these might be the last

private moments we will share with loved ones before the twin
hammers of isolation and solitude nail down each shady dawn.

The After Plants

Jane Rosenberg LaForge

Like weeds, the bougainvillea
are wanton, as our father found
the dandelions that demoralized
his gardening; their seeds dispersing
like salt tossed over the shoulder, or
something from which you might wrest
a serum. There are only two ways
to think about time once the divorce
is final: the facts as established on paper
and those of the ether. My mother
always hated the cypress installed
by the neighboring future divorcee
but held her tongue until after
my father left; with the after plants,
purple and rusted red, she found it
possible to assert her own perimeter.
On trellises they confronted
their own view to the canyon,
beyond the cypress's webbed panes,
like hook and ladder systems
that entangle fish, wrangling them
into martyrdom: what every divorced man
considers to be his fate in the dreams
of his release, yet finds them in daylight
to be his own singular vision.

Reception

Jane Rosenberg LaForge

The center of a sunflower is a parabolic curve.
I didn't copy this from some textbook,
but figured it out by looking at satellite dishes.
They crop up in Queens, the dishes do,
the outer-borough equivalent of kudzu,
relegated to terraces and roofs of second-
floor apartments meant to have a feel of
a real house, standing alone and proud,
a socially acceptable marking of territory.
I'm sorry. I hadn't meant this to be so angry.
I hadn't intended this to have so much form
or substance; only as an observation as to how
data is collected, stored for purposes of reproducing
stunning replicas. There are only so many shapes
in nature and everything else is Ecclesiastes;
a perfect circle comes with nary a deviation
from the original spectacle. My father's
hearing aids followed the shape of wasps' bellies,
heavy with wood, or the venom pumped into
arbitrary victims, the receiver species with
three fine bones and a gathering of hair,
lambent with sound, and shivering.

Choosing a Moon

Katie Manning

*"I think everybody in the poetry
community deserves their own moon."*
—Todd Dillard

Who can resist the pull
of Ganymede, the only
moon in the solar system
with its own magnetic field,
named for the most beautiful
boy? And don't most of us
make the mistake of taking
whatever is largest—a slice
of cake—or most lovely—
that gorgeous boy—even
when we know they're not
the best for us? Then I leap
to the other extreme: I think
of Deimos, smallest moon
of Mars, the 8-mile ball
I could keep in my cosmic
pocket, but who wants
to carry even a small
amount of dread? Then
I turn to Io, and my mouth
keeps turning the vowels
over and over. How could I
resist the liquid sounds
that label the driest object
in our solar system? How
can I help but see myself
in one of the few mortal
women beyond this earth?
What woman doesn't
contradict herself and

burn. The lava lakes
call to my tongue.
Io. This is the one.

This Poem is About Dinosaurs

Katie Manning

It is not about Jeff Goldblum. It is not
about how much I wanted him to run
his fingers gently over the back of my
hand and let a drop of water slip down
one way and then another while he
spoke softly to me about chaos theory
in that low rumble that God created—
surely—intentionally designed in that
man for seduction. I love dinosaurs.
I hung framed pictures of dinosaurs
around my bedroom and read so many
dinosaur books as a child. I definitely
watched *Jurassic Park* for the dinosaurs.
I definitely felt my whole body blush
when I heard Jeff Goldblum speak. I
didn't stop to think if I should. But
this is not about desire or about desire
locked behind electric gates, as if such
a force could ever be contained, as if I
could ever find a way to contain it.

Steger & Sons

Norman Minnick

There is an out-of-tune piano in the lobby
that everyone loves to play. The music one chooses
does not matter—it sounds like you've entered
a saloon in the Wild West in an old movie
and when someone walks in, the music stops.
Everyone turns to see the face of a stranger.
It wasn't always this way. When the piano was in tune
no one wanted to play.

The Show Must

Norman Minnick

Cloistered with a MacBook Air
I recorded everything I know
about William Shakespeare
while not wearing pants.
Due to a global pandemic
face-to-face classroom instruction
has been suspended.
We were in the middle of Othello
and Brianna was supposed to play
Desdemona, a role she had been
longing for all semester.
Despite 400 years of poverty,
hunger, genocide, war,
corruption, colonization, and disco,
honest Iago, that nemesis
most vile who wears his heart
upon his sleeve *for daws
to peck at*, will continue
to manipulate and destroy
the valiant Moor.

The House at the End of a Road

Richard Oyama

If your life is a leaf that the seasons tear off and condemn
They will bind you with love that is graceful and green as a stem
—Leonard Cohen

Last time I forgot my shoes.
This time feels a dream—
Half-invented, misremembered.

Her hands are soft and brisk
And drizzle oil. Can one
Ease into illusory flesh?

Is she maker of a secret craft?
What I want is opacity, a small death
To singe a hole in my blue polo shirt.

In this house at the end of a road
I change my life.

CALLIGRAPHY

Richard Oyama

The painting is a series of fire gestures,
Calligraphic circles, Zen scorings.

Sara Luisa reads me a poem on her cell:
"I think the mountain startled / my small grief."

Her reading has been a careering around
Loss. If you tempt the gods, Greta said,

They will smite you down. Epic tragedy
met by a glib and crimped smallness, the meticulous garden.

For years I made an ofrenda, she said, but how to
Elegize so many souls lost?

The body dissolves to ash, my life a sequence of
Fire gestures in the burning air.

In the Age of Losses

Dave Shumate

You don't realize you are in the age of losses until after the third death and the funeral director recognizes your voice on the telephone and starts calling you by your first name and the florist knows not to use gladioli in the arrangements and the police escorts stop just shy of saluting when you shuffle out of the mortuary and the children on the street stop singing nursery rhymes when you pick up the paper and the ice cream vendor turns his music off when he passes your house and the gravedigger stops shoveling long enough to reach up and remove his hat and hand you his business card.

In the Presence of Children

Dave Shumate

Generally speaking, it's good to have children around. Those purveyors of chaos and excavators of secrets. They lighten the mood. They stow themselves away in crevices and locate your suspenders or bra deep inside your drawers and convert them into weapons. They forge alliances and duel with forks. They watch the television preacher rant on and on and then concoct a religion of their own. They adopt people they encounter in dreams and introduce you to them in the morning. They invent new nations and appoint themselves ambassadors. They witness the neighborhood dogs mating and then raise the topic of sex at the dinner table. When you put them to bed, they babble on and on, then reach up and touch your cheek as if for the final time.

RIGHT OF RETURN

NEIL SILBERBLATT

You - moving your couch, or mowing
this olive grove -
you speak of your "right of return",
as though you knew the precise
address and apartment number
where Elijah left his things
before he ascended.

Even Isaac never returned home
after that afternoon.
Ishmael too – exiled with his mother –
was not allowed to come back and
re-claim his old bedroom.
But you, with your rake, shovel and bulldozer,
you claim this as your own.

You are a trespasser here.
You are the man so desperate for a bed,
that he breaks
into the wrong house.

See the woman and children asleep in their beds.
See the dishes in the sink.
That is not your wife.
Those are not your children.
Those are not your dishes.
And that is most certainly
not your olive grove.

Modern Times

Neil Silberblatt
(for my daughter, Zoe)

If given enough time,
I could show you
how it's done.

How, in Modern Times, Chaplin,
having secured a job -
during the great depression
which you've never heard of
but can look up -
as a night watchman in a department store,
roller-skated
blindfolded
of course, blindfolded
backwards
of course, backwards
ever closer to the floor's edge
about to fall to the floors below
to the shrieking delight of Paulette Goddard.

How the image of the cavernous drop
was super-imposed,
how Chaplin was never really in danger
beyond the myriad ways in which
anyone skating backwards
and blindfolded
is in danger.

I could show you
how Harold Lloyd managed to climb
that clock tower
without plummeting to the street below,
or how Keaton did anything.

But I won't.
Not because I am cruel,
but because I love you
and want you to
shriek with Paulette
each time he gets close
to the edge.

Animal Dreams

Meghan Sterling

I am ready to be every animal—crocodile, koala, skink, lemur.
I dream my skin is scales, fur, feathers, a tenderer cover.
I dream I walk the streets of Rome with my hoofs sharp
against cobblestones, that I am curled beside the radiator,
my tail as pillow, my ears alive. I am ready to be every animal

that didn't survive my ownership—a rabbit that ate its way out
of a metal cage, a borrowed hamster, a dog that turned out to be
vicious, a wild cat we thought we could contain. I see the rows
of tombstones in the pet cemetery down the street: Bailey, Cleo,
Maple, Buddy, Max, and I dream I am living the simple life

of the petted—sleep, wake, eat from a bowl, business outside,
play. And again. And again. And then, confronting my owner
in punctuations of love, the silent nearness. I dream I am a cat
held in a lap and the heat is love. I dream I am a goldfish
and the magnified eyes watching me over the glass bowl's lip

are love. I am ready to love everything like that,
the way a dog will nudge a ball with its nose over towards
its owner's feet, the way a cat will paw at one bright spot of sun
on the floor, circle it twice, and settle into light.

Rear-View

Meghan Sterling

And then you come to realize that you have chosen your life,
where instead of croissants in your 19th-century Parisian walkup

it's cheerios and sippy cups, soon to be backpacks
and soccer cleats, followed by lip balm and mall drop-offs.

You aren't questioning what's next anymore—examining maps
of the Pacific Northwest to see where a random move could take you,

scrolling ads for camper-vans or Airstreams, searching crowds
for the eyes of your life-companion—you have found him

and he sleeps hard, his face deep in a pillow as you write this.
You know now that all the waffling about having a baby

was just an attempt to create a fork in the road. Should I? Should I?
The question itself was your answer. And sure, you used to scamper

to Peru or Vietnam or Mexico or Europe easily, quickly,
packing your tattered Lonely Planets and ripe hiking boots,

those unfamiliar cities and landscapes bright as the wings of birds,
your solitude mirrored in the vistas you encountered, Lake Como

and Lucerne spilling all that blue at your feet, alone in the present tense,
your skin vivid with new light. Only now it's the little things

that send you careening, like the apartment empty for a few hours
this morning, almost too much in the vastness it offers—

sunlight hovering like a white moth, the memory of the turn
you didn't take.

BUFFALO JUMP

SUSAN TERRIS

*"There is a light breaking through the storm
And it is buffalo hunting weather."
—Joy Harjo,* The Story Wheel

Close your eyes. Don't open them until I say it's okay.
Our story wheel starts to turn, as we step away from

the Rocky Mountain Bierstadt's and into the haze,
fog-shrouded plain with the herd of buffalo. Can't tell
you how we got here, but we are among them. They are

quiet, watchful, placid, enormous yet with delicate
legs, spiked hoofs and each one oddly solitary.
We're small, phantom-like, neither welcomed nor

shunned. Then without warning through the mist,
dust clouds and sound of horses hoofs, men howling.
Panicked, the herd is chuffing, snorting, wild-eyed.

As are we. Desperate, we do as Odysseus once
did, bend, grab onto hairy bellies and hold tight.
Blindly, the herd charges through fog,

flight-not-fight from the enemy, past the flat plain
into a rock-walled canyon, then driven toward
the edge of a cliff. There, buffalo skid, collide.

We fall. I open my eyes. And you can open yours.
We're sprawled on end-grain of the Denver gallery,
near Bierstadt's Estes Peak. And by our painting.

We see its dark turf, thick fog. But no buffalo.
All vanished. Not even their shadows left behind.

***

The painting "Herd of Buffalo," 1862 by William Jacob Hayes
Denver Art Museum

THE PURKAPILE TEST

SUSAN TERRIS

In *Spoon River Anthology,* Mr. Purkapile comes
home after a gap year and tells his wife—alas—he
was captured by pirates on Lake Michigan.

What if I'd returned a year after I set out for
a 4-day conference in Chicago and told my spouse
I'd been kidnapped by pirates on the lake?

He'd have put his arms around me, welcomed
me back, never once asking if I'd been with
that pipe-smoking poet who knows Yeats by heart

and me also. My spouse would have been loving,
loyal, and would have wanted to punish the pirates
by beating them with his pool cue. And still,

what if I'd been Mrs. Purkapile and my husband had
returned after a year with the same crazy pirate
taradiddle? Would I have asked about the cruelties

he'd endured, the chills, the chains, the gang rape? No.
I would have been gone, living in sin with the poet
who knows *things fall apart and the centre cannot hold.*

ARTIFACT

Cindy Veach

An eighth-grader in Colorado found a T-Rex tooth on a hike.
It looked like a plain rock, a little shiny. After he rinsed it off
he knew and emailed the Denver Museum of Nature and Science.
Imagine, a sixty-million-year old tooth in the dirt of a county
full of strip malls and cul-de-sacs, not even buried but right out
in the open and an eighth-grade boy just walking along
wearing his backpack. Is this a good time to bring up birds?
How they're descended from dinosaurs. Mini, manageable
monsters: beaked and clawed, scales turned to feathers
and roars to song. Since kindergarten the boy practiced lockdowns,
learned how to hide, play dead until it became as natural
as brushing his teeth. Once in a while, the alchemy
of monsters works in our favor. Once in a while
there is good news. A living boy. His rare find.

How to Mourn a Dead Icelandic Glacier from Massachusetts

Cindy Veach

When you live in an apartment right on the street.
When all you have is a shoebox-sized porch
and one whiskey barrel planter with a single sprout
eking up smack in the middle, you drag your folding

chair out there and sit, both feet propped on the rail
and listen hard, curve your ears around car noise until
you hear a bird somewhere in the neighborhood
maybe an emboldened turkey down by the cemetery

corralling his crew, or a murder of crows advancing
toward a nugget of squirrel guts a few blocks away.
Even if you can't see it with your own eyes
you know enough to celebrate this iota of wildness

in a cityscape far from Iceland where today
they're grieving a glacier killed on your watch.

I Dressed My Salad with Sadness

Cindy Veach

Yesterday, as I cubed an English hothouse cucumber,
sliced red-eyed radishes, grated a baby carrot

and my knuckle, I thought of my sister in Pennsylvania.
Remembered us making lunch together a year ago,

before the virus. Remembered sharing her Cutco knife,
her pig shaped cutting board, the last rich chunk

of Hass avocado. I'm not brave. I winced for my knuckle.
It was my hands that remembered the two of us

standing shoulder to shoulder at her kitchen counter,
chatting about a movie we'd watched, her dogs begging

at our knees. A mundane moment, a moment
that would have been forgotten any other year.

Before I knew it everyone I missed got tossed into that salad:
my sister, my kids, my mother, dear friends, the grandchild

I've yet to meet. It was a magnificent salad! Epic, five star—
and I let myself sob it down sitting alone at my kitchen counter,

chewing with my mouth open, dressing dribbling down my chin.

NAUSICAA, AGORA

ALLISON WILKINS

There's no reason to think of you here
among the captured fish, rigid on ice.
The vendors have set a good market price—
but passing the squid, I think of your spear
gun, then your wife, pregnant again.
She hopes the baby will make you warmer;
children's wooden toys around the corner.
I wonder this too, every now and then.
I pick up a miniature horse-painted
bowl. Perfect size for a little one's hands.
It won't happen for me, I understand.
Lover, you asked me and so I waited.
Another kiss. Despair. Our empty mouths.
Like fish gradually drowning on our air.

***"Nausicaa, Agora" begins with a line from Lexi Rudnitsky's "Epilogue: Phoenix Revisited."

Reviews

Reviews

I Was a Bell
by M. Soledad Caballero
(Red Hen Press, 2021)

Reviewed by Elizabeth Nichols

M. Soledad Caballero's *I Was a Bell* impressively tackles complex, interconnected subjects of memory, the immigration experience, generational trauma, and the search for identity. Through the speaker in her poems, Caballero recollects her experiences as a young child escaping the violent coup in Chile under Augusto Pinochet. Caballero does not shy away from the reality of the coup, detailing the horrific loss of life and survivors' trauma. The collection explores her family's immigration experience from Chile to Oklahoma, the silencing of her culture therein, and the struggle to reclaim her sense of self in spite of generational trauma and her own illness. Caballero's strong narrative voice is supported by evocative imagery that recurs throughout the collection, heightening the reader's understanding of the speaker's emotional journey. Birds, silence, song, shadows, and light reappear again and again throughout the collection, revealing the inescapable interconnectedness between past and present. Through Caballero's raw testimony of her experience and unflinching resolve to recover her sense of cultural identity and self, *I Was a Bell* demonstrates that the "snarl of memory" can be unwound to make sense of the emotional and physical weight of human experience.

Birds are embedded into the pages of *I Was a Bell*. Their tracks guide the reader visually through the poems—printed in sinuous gray paths behind bold stanzas and lines—while also nesting into the bedrock of the collection's metaphors and imagery. The image of the bird is at its most powerful when it is connected to the speaker herself. In "Bird Girl," for example, the speaker reckons with her inner child. "Bird girl," she asks, "who took you bird girl who made you so / small we could not find you with any words or guns or people or stories or secrets or / love, who made you so small." This poem recalls the images in "Birds of Prey," in which the speaker describes her grandmother's kept birds and her childhood interactions with them. "Some days," the speaker recalls, "I hid in the cage," and held a bird in her hands for hours in spite of grandmother's chiding to leave it alone. Holding the bird in her hands was a comforting respite from the "soldiers' boots and guns, the

63

green tanks on the streets, the silence and hunger" of the coup. Her child-self desperately clutched the bird in her hands, "crushing [her] bird with hope." The image of the speaker as child holding the bird poignantly parallels the reckoning the speaker has with her inner child in "Bird Girl," as if the adult speaker is holding her child self in hands, mourning some hope lost, yearning for a lost sense of self: "Half her life, she has been gone silence. In silence, in the darkness, who took her, who disappeared this girl willowy and sweet?"

Silence is a recurring theme in *I Was a Bell*, and stands in diametrical opposition to the theme of song. In Caballero's work, silence is both a symptom and a survival strategy born of the trauma of the past. The speaker's mother is silent about the years of coup and blood under Pinochet, her "memories mute about the decades of sadness" while her father's silence is of tangled syllables that hold "secrets like underground roots." There is also a silencing of culture described throughout the collection, as deftly detailed in poems such as "Losing Spanish," "My English Decades," and "Memory Spaces." In particular, "Memory Spaces" poignantly illustrates this silencing of identity and culture:

> *We never asked why we could not speak*
> *Spanish. We just didn't. Even if it was stuck,*
> *a wedge in our throats, a piece of our planet left*
> *behind, secret, not wanted. At the dinner table,*
> *there was a secret universe, like galaxies that shine*
> *and flicker to get attention. We let the whole world*
> *grow gray, rather than love in the colors of the past.*
> *Secret. Shameful, that tangle of vowels and accents.*

While this silence was an effective tool of survival through the traumas of political violence and immigration, it chafes against the speaker. She challenges the supposed wisdom of silence in the poem "After the Election: A Father Speaks to His Son." The father tries to reassure his son, promising that the newly elected populist and his radicalized followers will not come for them. He tells his son, "…we are the quiet kind, the ones / who stay late and do not speak…. / He says, we are safe in silence." Recalling the horror of Pinochet's coup, the speaker counters that so many, "tried to stay thin, be small, tried / breaking bone and voice…. To be still enough to be left alone. …. / It never works. To become nothing. / They come for the shadows, too." Finally, the speaker faces her own struggle with perpetuating silence in the last poem of the collection, "Rooted." While rejoicing in the birth of a new family member, she captures the feeling of renewal warring against buried intergenerational trauma:

> *…She would be the new*
> *world. We all saw our bright planet in her small*
> *blue eyes, curly hair. We did not want to see*
> *any accents or sadness. She would be the door,*
> *she would be the gate, she would be the whole*
> *to our brokenness. This is how the muting*
> *continues. We contort. We twist ourselves.*
> *We aspire to quiet space in between cracks.*

But as she matures, this new family member "has no patience for quiet immigrants." She, much like the speaker in previous poems, chafes against the silence, raging "against / the emptiness of bootstraps and hidden shames." She demands of her older relatives, "What am I? Who am I?" Her demands echo the speaker's own search for identity in the memories of the past, in the "songs before English." In her young family member's defiance of silence, the collection closes on a note of cultural recovery and hope.

The memories in *I Was a Bell* also defy silence. They recall song and color with vivid flushes of imagery and culture. Memory leads to an emotional grappling with the experiences that radically changed the speaker's identity and family, and ultimately leads to a rediscovery of self. Stories from the past inform a reclaiming of the speaker's voice—her song. In "What it Takes," the speaker makes this defiance of silence tangible and actionable: "It is going to take bodies, it always does. / … Bodies carry the world and the weight of sorrow / and song. It takes so many voices, / millions of sounding voices in the sky, / …to ring, to rise / to breathe song into the silence." Indeed, the voices and stories of those that survived the coup—the memories of those that ran, fought, bled and died—reverberate in I Was a Bell, engendering a kind of raising of millions voices that the speaker calls for in "What it Takes."

65

At the conclusion of Caballero's *I Was a Bell*, in other words, the speaker is no longer "lost / between stories" and memories, but found in them.

Prompts

Francesca Bell

Perhaps because I have a disordered relationship to anxiety, the prompt that most reliably, richly works for me is to ask myself the question, "What are you afraid of," and free-write from there.

Ace Boggess

Write about someplace you've never been, but imagine it as a mythic earthly paradise.

Rebecca Brock

When you first wake, what tells you that you are home—either home in your bed or home in your body? The shape of your feet? The lump of the dog breathing? The way the light falls?

Lauren K. Carlson

Create a pattern, and then disrupt it. Try this by writing about an occurrence that happens with regularity: morning coffee, doing the dishes, pumping gas, checking the weather. Then insert an unusual or oppositional force. What happens next?

Julia Chiapella

This is a prompt courtesy of the inimitable Tony Hoagland: consider opening a poem with an admission of failure, either personal, professional, minor, or major. Experiment with writing out of a voice (your own) that admits fault and see where the poem goes after that. Strive to be blunt and un-self-flattering.

H. Lee Coakley

Write a poem that is a funhouse reflection of something that was a part of your day today—an object, person, interaction, memory, dream, or event. How might it get distorted? How does that distortion show up in the poem?

Steven Deutsch

Nostos, basically homecoming.
I found this word the other day.
Makes me think of memory, often an element in reading and writing poetry—and isn't a memory but a homecoming of sorts.

Sherine Gilmour

Find a source of language that is unusual or contrasts with your poetic language. This might be a history book, medical research, an online hobby group, etc. Write a poem in which you explore a part of yourself using this language.

Joan Kwon Glass

In her poem 'The Uses of Sorrow,' Mary Oliver wrote: 'Someone I loved once gave me / a box full of darkness / it took me years to understand / that this too, was a gift.' Pretend that Mary is standing before you, holding open your box of darkness; write an epistolary poem about what it contains.

Max Heinegg

When I'm in a rut, I like to replace all the words to the melody of a song, or try to mirror the flow of a rapper by typing "instrumental of..." into YouTube, and writing along. It's a low-key and playful way to work with metrics and rhyme without feeling too formal. Just don't embarrass yourself by reading it to your students like I do!

Tim Kahl

1) Write a letter to the word "if" and thank it for its service to the contingent world, then encourage it to have more confidence and be more definitive in the future.

2) Pretend that you are writing a TV commercial for a human emotion. What would you say to your viewing audience to get them to experience this emotion? Would your commercial look and feel like a poem itself?

Jen Karetnick

Write a 17-syllable American sentence (as per Allen Ginsberg's definition). Then use each word of that sentence vertically as the first word of a line for a poem.

Jane Rosenberg LaForge

Take any news event and think back to when something like this happened when you were younger; preferably when you were very much younger, perhaps too young to understand all the ins and outs of said event. How do you remember that event, and how has your perception about it changed, in light of your now-adult understanding of the news, yourself, and the world?

Katie Manning

Write a poem with the title, "This Poem Is about _____," filling in the blank with something that captures your imagination and has symbolic value for you, perhaps something you've wanted to write about but haven't been able to yet. Then draft a poem that insists it is not about other topics, and see where those negations take you.

Norman Minnick

Write about walking in on your parents....

Richard Oyama

Upend the contents of the poem by reversing the order of the lines, i.e. the last line is first, the penultimate line is second and so on. In other words, you shake up the predictability and direction of the poem by turning it upside down (credit to Kathleen Fraser, my late poetry teacher at San Francisco State University, for this prompt).

Dave Shumate

Conversations with the Dead—most of Sappho's surviving work consists of intriguing and suggestive poetic fragments. Begin a writing session by composing a fragment of a poem an ancient, imaginary poet might have left behind. Let the fragment sit for a while. Then playfully begin experimenting, as a modern poet, with filling in the rest of the poem: playfully being the operative word.

Neil Silberblatt

"...to die is different from what anyone supposed, and luckier" (Whitman).

Meghan Sterling

What is something or someone else you would like to embody—for a day, a week, a lifetime? A leaf, a fish, a child, Prime Minister of Malta? Choose ten words from any poem in this book. Start with the phrase, "I'm ready to be every ___ there ever was," fill in the blank with a word of your own, and then weave the ten words into a poem about another life you could live.

Susan Terris

Write a five-line poem that has a month, a color, a person or animal, a place you've never been, and one sentence about yourself.

Cindy Veach

Look out a window and write down the first five things you notice. Next, write down a news item, preferably something odd or quirky. Now write a 14-line poem that incorporates the items you've written down. Be sure to include a volta in the poem.

Allison Wilkins

Recycling: mine your abandoned drafts by looking for phrases and lines that seem to speak to each other or share a common theme. Paste the salvaged words or phrases into a new document and see what happens. For added fun, impose a form (sonnets and sestinas are my favorites) or a persona.

Contributor Notes

Francesca Bell's debut collection, *Bright Stain* (Red Hen Press, 2019), was a finalist for the Washington State Book Award and Julie Suk Award. Her second collection, *What Small Sound* will be published in 2023, as will her translation of Max Sessner's collection, *Kitchens and Trains*, both by Red Hen Press. Bell's work appears in *Alaska Quarterly Review, New Ohio Review, North American Review, Mid-American Review*, and *Rattle*.

Ace Boggess is the author of six books of poetry, most recently *Escape Envy* (Brick Road Poetry Book, 2021). His poems have appeared in *Michigan Quarterly Review, South Carolina Review, North Dakota Quarterly, Notre Dame Review*, and other journals. An ex-con, he lives in Charleston, West Virginia, where he writes and tries to stay out of trouble.

Rebecca Brock's work appears in *The Threepenny Review, CALYX, The Comstock Review, Whale Road Review* and elsewhere. She was a finalist in the 2021 Joy Harjo Poetry Contest at *Cutthroat* and won the 2022 Editor's Choice Award at *Sheila-Na-Gig*. She is a reader at *SWWIM Everyday*. Her chapbook, *Each Bearing Out*, will be available this fall from Kelsay Books. Idaho-born, she has lived in Virginia for nearly two decades. You can find more of her work at rebeccabrock.org.

Lauren K. Carlson is the author of the chapbook *Animals I Have Killed*. Recent work forthcoming from *Salamander Mag, Waxwing,* and *Ploughshares*. She is a graduate of the Warren Wilson MFA Program for Writers and a reader for Palette Poetry.

Julia Chiapella's poetry has appeared in *Avatar Review, Edison Literary Review, I-70 Review, The MacGuffin, Midwest Quarterly, OPEN: Journal of Arts & Letters, The Opiate Magazine,* and *The Wax Paper* among others. She co-founded Santa Cruz Writes to enhance literary opportunities for Santa Cruz County, California residents. The retired director of the Young Writers Program, which she established in 2012, Julia received the Gail Rich Award in 2017 for creative contributions to Santa Cruz County.

H. Lee Coakley (they/she) is a Queer poet and nutritional healer currently based in Brooklyn, NY. They hold a BA from New York University and an MSPH from Johns Hopkins University. Their work has been featured in *Lavender Review, Red Eft Review, Utterance Journal, The Voices Project, Blueshift Anthology* and *The Mad Farmer Reading Series.*

Steve Deutsch lives in State College, PA. Some of his recent publications have or will appear in *MacQueens Quinterly, Santa Clara Review, Sangam, Poetica Review, Lothlorien, Muddy River Poetry Review, Silver Birch, Backchannels, Red Weather, The Drabble, Sheila-na-gig, The Rush, Pirene's Fountain, Evening Street Review,* and *Schuylkill Valley Journal.* He is poetry editor of *Centered Magazine.* Deutsch was nominated three times for the Pushcart Prize. His chapbook, *Perhaps You Can,* was published in 2019 by Kelsay Press. His full length book, *Persistence of Memory,* was published in 2020 by Kelsay. Deutsch's third book of poetry, *Going, Going, Gone,* was published in 2021.

Sherine Gilmour has an M.F.A. in Creative Writing from New York University (1999). She was nominated for Best New Poets 2020 and a Pushcart Prize. Her poetry, essays, and fiction have been published or are forthcoming from *Cleaver, Entropy, Mom Egg Review, Redivider, So To Speak, Third Coast,* and other publications.

Joan Kwon Glass is the mixed-race, Korean American author of *Night Swim* (Diode Editions, 2022) and three chapbooks. She serves as Editor-in-Chief for *Harbor Review*, as a Brooklyn Poets Mentor, is a proud Smith College graduate and has been a public school educator for 20 years. Her work has won or been finalist for several prizes and her poems have been nominated for the Pushcart Prize and Sundress Anthology *Best of the Net*. Kwon Glass' poems have been published or are forthcoming in *Prairie Schooner, RHINO, Rattle, The Rupture, Dialogist* and elsewhere. She lives in Connecticut with her family.

Max Heinegg is the author of *Good Harbor* (forthcoming spring 2022), which won the inaugural Paul Nemser Prize from Lily Poetry Press. His poems have appeared in *32 Poems, Thrush, The Cortland Review, Nimrod,* and *Columbia Poetry Review.* He has been nominated for *Best of the Net* and the Pushcart Prize; won the Sidney Lanier poetry prize and Emily Stauffer poetry prize; and has been a finalist for the poetry prizes of *Crab Creek Review, December Magazine, Cultural Weekly, Cutthroat, Rougarou, Asheville Poetry Review,* the Nazim Hikmet Prize, and *Twyckenham* By day, he is a high school English teacher and singer-songwriter; and by night, a recording artist whose records can be heard at www.maxheinegg.com

Tim Kahl http://www.timkahl.com is the author of *Possessing Yourself* (CW Books, 2009), *The Century of Travel* (CW Books, 2012), *The String of Islands* (Dink, 2015) and *Omnishambles* (Bald Trickster, 2019). His work has been published in *Prairie Schooner, Drunken Boat, Mad Hatters' Review, Indiana Review, Metazen, Ninth Letter, Sein und Werden, Notre Dame Review, The Really System, Konundrum Engine Literary Magazine, The Journal, The Volta, Parthenon West Review, Caliban* and many other journals in the U.S. He is also editor of *Clade Song* http://www.cladesong.com. He is the vice president and events coordinator of The Sacramento Poetry Alliance. He also has a public installation in Sacramento (*In Scarcity We Bare The Teeth*). He plays flutes, guitars, ukuleles, charangos and cavaquinhos. He currently teaches at California State University, Sacramento, where he sings lieder while walking on campus between classes.

Jen Karetnick's most recent collection, *The Burning Where Breath Used to Be* (David Robert Books, 2020), is a CIPA EVVY winner, an Eric Hoffer Poetry Category finalist and a Kops Fetherling honorable mention. Her fifth full-length book is forthcoming from Salmon Poetry in 2023. The co-founder and managing editor of *SWWIM Every Day*, she has work appearing recently or forthcoming in *The Comstock Review, Matter, Michigan Quarterly Review, The Shore,* and *Under a Warm Green Linden*. See jkaretnick.com.

Jane Rosenberg LaForge's next full-length poetry collection, including essays, will be *My Aunt's Abortion from BlazeVOX* [Books] in 2023. Her most recent novel, *Sisterhood of the Infamous* (New Meridian Arts Press 2021), was a finalist in the National Indie Excellence Awards in regional fiction (West). More poetry is forthcoming in *Evening Street Review* and an anthology to be published by Bell Press Books.

Katie Manning is the founding editor-in-chief of *Whale Road Review* and a professor of writing in San Diego. She is the author of *Tasty Other*, which won the 2016 Main Street Rag Poetry Book Award, and her fifth chapbook, *28,065 Nights*, is available from River Glass Books. Her poems have appeared in *December, The Lascaux Review, New Letters, Poet Lore,* and many other venues; and her poem "What to Expect" was recently featured on the *Poetry Unbound* podcast from The On Being Project. Find her online at www.katiemanningpoet.com.

Norman Minnick is the author of three collections of poetry, most recently *Advice for a Young Poet*. He is the editor of *Between Water and Song: New Poets for the Twenty-First Century* and *The Lost Etheridge: Uncollected Poems of Etheridge Knight*, forthcoming in 2022. Visit www.buzzminnick.com for more information.

Richard Oyama's work has appeared in *Premonitions: The Kaya Anthology of New Asian North American Poetry, The Nuyorasian Anthology, Breaking Silence, Dissident Song, A Gift of Tongues, About Place, Konch Magazine, Pirene's Fountain, Tribes, Malpais Review, Anak Sastra, Buddhist Poetry Review* and other literary journals. *The Country They Know* (Neuma Books, 2005) is his first collection of poetry. He has a M.A. in English: Creative Writing from San Francisco State University. Oyama taught at California College of Arts in Oakland, University of California at Berkeley and University of New Mexico. His first novel in a trilogy, *A Riot Goin' On,* is forthcoming.

David Shumate is the author of three books of prose poems published by the University of Pittsburgh Press: *Kimonos in the Closet* (2013), *The Floating Bridge* (2008) and *High Water Mark* (2004), winner of the 2003 Agnes Lynch Starrett Poetry Prize. His poetry has appeared widely in literary journals and has been anthologized in *Good Poems for Hard Times, The Best American Poetry,* and *The Writer's Almanac* as well as in numerous anthologies and university texts. Shumate is a lecturer in Butler University's MFA program, and he lives in Zionsville, Indiana.

Neil Silberblatt's poems have appeared in numerous journals, including *The American Journal of Poetry, Tikkun Daily, Cutthoat, Tiferet Journal, Plume Poetry Journal, Lily Poetry Review, Mom Egg Review,* and *Naugatuck River Review.* His work has been selected for various anthologies, including *Collateral Damage* (*Pirene's Fountain*) and *Culinary Poems* (Glass Lyre Press). His most recent poetry book, *Past Imperfect* (Nixes Mate Books, 2018), was nominated for the Mass. Book Award in Poetry and he has been nominated several times for a Pushcart Prize.

Silberblatt is the founder/director of Voices of Poetry. Since 2012, he has curated/organized more than 400 VOP events, featuring acclaimed poets and writers (including several Poets Laureate and Pulitzer Prize winners/finalists) at various venues, including The Mount/Edith Wharton's home in Lenox, MA; Chesterwood in Stockbridge, MA; McNally Jackson Books in NYC; and Ike & Randy's Boxing Gym in Paterson, NJ. Silberblatt has been the recipient of grants from the Massachusetts Cultural Council. In his spare time, he battles Stage IV metastatic colon cancer.

Meghan Sterling lives and teaches workshops in Portland, Maine. Her work has been published or is forthcoming in *Rattle, Rust & Moth, SWWIM, The Night Heron Barks, Cider Press Review, Inflectionist Review, Sky Island Journal, Westchester Review, Pine Hills Review, Mom Egg Review* and many others. She is Associate

Poetry Editor of the *Maine Review,* and winner of Sweet Literary's 2021 annual poetry contest. Her collection *These Few Seeds* is out now from Terrapin Books. Read her work at meghansterling.com.

Susan Terris' recent books are *Familiar Tense* (Marsh Hawk, 2019), *Take Two: Film Studies* (Omnidawn) 2017, *Memos* (Omnidawn, 2015), and *Ghost of Yesterday: New & Selected Poems* (Marsh Hawk, 2012). She is the author of seven books of poetry, 17 chapbooks, three artists' books, and two plays. Journals include *The Southern Review, Georgia Review, Prairie Schooner, Blackbird,* and *Ploughshares.* A poem of hers appeared in *Pushcart Prize XXXI.* A poem from *Memos* was in *Best American Poetry 2015.* Her newest book is *Dream Fragments,* which won the 2019 Swan Scythe Press Award. Terris is editor emerita of *Spillway Magazine* and a poetry editor at *Pedestal.* www.susanterris.com

Cindy Veach is the author of *Her Kind* (CavanKerry Press), a finalist for the 2022 Eric Hoffer Montaigne Medal; *Gloved Against Blood* (CavanKerry Press), a finalist for the Paterson Poetry Prize and a Massachusetts Center for the Book 'Must Read;' and the chapbook, *Innocents* (Nixes Mate). Her poems have appeared in the *Academy of American Poets Poem-a-Day, AGNI, Michigan Quarterly Review, Poet Lore* and *Salamander* among others. Veach is the recipient of the Philip Booth Poetry Prize and the Samuel Allen Washington Prize. She is co-poetry editor of *MER (Mom Egg Review).* www.cindyveach.com

Allison Wilkins is the assistant director for Writing Workshops in Greece. Her first book of poems, *Girl Who,* was published by CW Books. Her poems and essays have appeared in *Hayden's Ferry Review, Superstition Review, Birmingham Poetry Review, Michigan Quarterly* and others.

Glass Lyre Press

exceptional works to replenish the spirit

Glass Lyre Press is an independent literary publisher interested in technically accomplished, stylistically distinct, and original work. Glass Lyre seeks diverse writers that possess a dynamic aesthetic and an ability to emotionally and intellectually engage a wide audience of readers.

Glass Lyre's vision is to connect the world through language and art. We hope to expand the scope of poetry and short fiction for the general reader through exceptionally well-written books, which evoke emotion, provide insight, and resonate with the human spirit.

Poetry Collections
Poetry Chapbooks
Select Short & Flash Fiction
Anthologies

www.GlassLyrePress.com

www.ingramcontent.com/pod-product-compliance
Lightning Source LLC
Chambersburg PA
CBHW030350100526

44592CB00010B/898